KS1
5–7
Years

G000298891

Master Maths at Home

Extra Challenges

Scan the QR code to help your child's learning at home.

  | **MATHS**
NO PROBLEM!

mastermathsathome.com

How to use this book

Maths — No Problem! created **Master Maths at Home** to help children develop fluency in the subject and a rich understanding of core concepts.

Key features of the Master Maths at Home books include:

- Carefully designed lessons that provide structure, but also allow flexibility in how they're used. For example, some children may want to write numbers, while others might want to trace.

- Speech bubbles containing content designed to spark diverse conversations, with many discussion points that don't have obvious 'right' or 'wrong' answers.

- Rich illustrations that will guide children to a discussion of shapes and units of measurement, allowing them to make connections to the wider world around them.

- Exercises that allow a flexible approach and can be adapted to suit any child's cognitive or functional ability.

- Clearly laid-out pages that encourage children to practise a range of higher-order skills.

- A community of friendly and relatable characters who introduce each lesson and come along as your child progresses through the series.

You can see more guidance on how to use these books at **mastermathsathome.com**.

We're excited to share all the ways you can learn maths!

Copyright © 2022 Maths — No Problem!

Maths — No Problem!
mastermathsathome.com
www.mathsnoproblem.com
hello@mathsnoproblem.com

First published in Great Britain in 2022 by
Dorling Kindersley Limited
One Embassy Gardens, 8 Viaduct Gardens, London SW11 7BW
A Penguin Random House Company

The authorised representative in the EEA is Dorling Kindersley
Verlag GmbH. Amulfstr. 124, 80636 Munich, Germany

10 9 8 7 6 5 4 3 2
003–327072–Jan/22

A CIP catalogue record for this book is available from the British Library.

ISBN: 978-0-24153-915-6
Printed and bound in the UK

For the curious
www.dk.com

This book was made with Forest Stewardship Council™ certified paper - one small step in DK's commitment to a sustainable future. For more information go to www.dk.com/our-green-pledge

Acknowledgements
The publisher would like to thank the authors and consultants Andy Psarianos, Judy Hornigold, Adam Gifford and Dr Anne Hermanson.

The Castledown typeface has been used with permission from the Colophon Foundry.

Contents

Ruby   Elliott   Amira   Charles   Lulu   Sam   Oak   Holly   Ravi   Emma   Jacob   Hannah

Comparing numbers

Starter

Emma uses [2], [1] and [3] to write three 2-digit numbers.

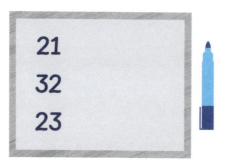

Which is the smallest number?

Example

tens	ones
2	1

tens	ones
3	2

tens	ones
2	3

3 tens is more than 2 tens.

32 is greater than 21. 32 > 21

32 is greater than 23. 32 > 23

32 is the greatest number.

23 is greater than 21. 23 > 21

21 is the smallest number.

The tens are the same, compare the ones next.

1 Use 4 , 3 and 5 to write:

(a) the greatest 2-digit number ☐

(b) the smallest 2-digit number ☐

2 Use 8 , 4 and 6 to write two different 2-digit numbers.

Use the numbers to fill in the blanks.

☐ < ☐

Is there more than one answer?

3 Use 7 , 5 and 6 to write six different 2-digit numbers.

Put the numbers in order, starting with the greatest.

☐ , ☐ , ☐ , ☐ , ☐ , ☐

4 (a) Fill in the blanks on the number line using the following numbers.

59, 72, 63, 54, 85, 77

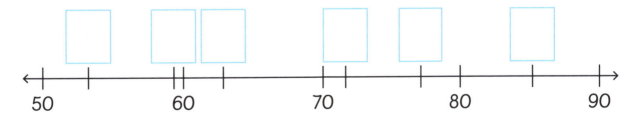

(b) Compare the numbers using > or <.

63 ☐ 59   77 ☐ 85

54 ☐ 72   72 ☐ 77

Solving addition problems

Starter

There are 26 children in the sports club.
There are 37 children in the arts club.
How many children are in the clubs altogether?

Example

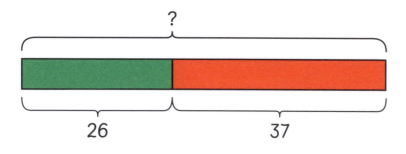

$$
\begin{array}{r}
{}^{1}2\ \ 6 \\
+\ \ 3\ \ 7 \\
\hline
3 \\
\hline
\end{array}
\qquad
\begin{array}{r}
{}^{1}2\ \ 6 \\
+\ \ 3\ \ 7 \\
\hline
6\ \ 3 \\
\hline
\end{array}
$$

Add the ones.

Then add the tens.

26 + 37 = 63

There are 63 children in the clubs altogether.

1 Charles read 37 pages of a book on Monday.
He read 45 pages of the book on Tuesday.
How many pages did he read over the two days?

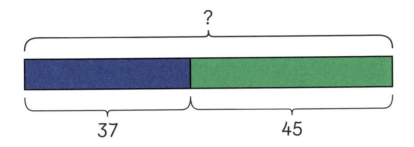

Charles read ⬚ pages over the two days.

2 Class 2A has 56 books in their class library.
Class 2B has 39 books in their class library.
How many books do the two classes have altogether?

The two classes have ⬚ books altogether.

Solving subtraction problems

Starter

There are 53 passengers on a train.
When the train stops, 28 passengers get off.
How many passengers are left on the train?

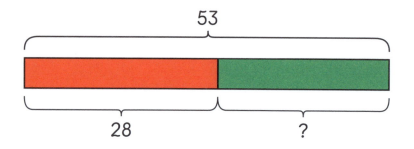

Example

$$\begin{array}{r} {\scriptstyle 4}{\scriptstyle 13} \\ \cancel{5}\ \cancel{3} \\ -\ 2\ \ 8 \\ \hline 5 \end{array}$$

$$\begin{array}{r} {\scriptstyle 4}{\scriptstyle 13} \\ \cancel{5}\ \cancel{3} \\ -\ 2\ \ 8 \\ \hline 2\ \ 5 \end{array}$$

Rename 1 ten as 10 ones, then subtract the ones.

Subtract the tens.

53 − 28 = 25

There are 25 passengers left on the train.

1 There are 63 children in the school hall.
37 children leave to go back to their classrooms.
How many children are still in the hall?

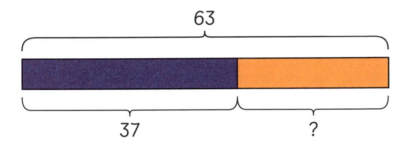

There are [ ] children still in the hall.

2 82 children start a sponsored run.
After an hour, 48 children have finished the run.
How many children have not yet finished the run?

[ ] children have not yet finished the run.

Solving multiplication problems

Starter

Holly uses 15 cm of ribbon to make a flower. How much ribbon does she need to make 3 flowers?

Example

Each flower needs 15 cm of ribbon.
There are 3 flowers.

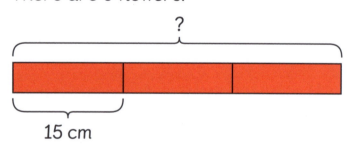

15 cm

$10 \times 3 = 30$
$5 \times 3 = 15$

's method:

$15 + 15 + 15 = 45$

's method:

$15 \times 3 = 45$

Holly needs 45 cm of ribbon to make 3 flowers.

Which method do you prefer?
Which method would be better to find out how much ribbon is needed to make 10 flowers?

1 Ruby places 10 identical straws in a straight line. Each straw is 8 cm long. What is the total length of the 10 straws?

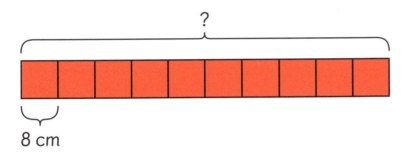

8 cm

The total length of the 10 straws is ☐ cm.

2 Emma stacks 9 identical books. Each book is 5 cm thick. What is the height of the stack of 9 books?

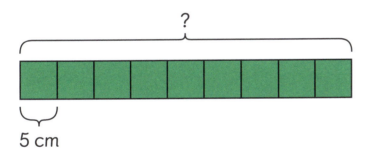

5 cm

The height of the stack of 9 books is ☐ cm.

3 Sam cuts a strip of paper into 5 equal pieces. Each piece is 7 cm long. What was the length of the strip of paper to begin with?

The length of the strip of paper was ☐ cm to begin with.

Solving division problems

Starter

A farmer is building a fence that is 10 m long. He uses 5 identical fence panels. How long is each fence panel?

Example

Do we multiply or divide?

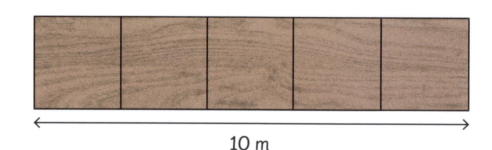

10 m

$10 \div 5 = 2$

Each fence panel is 2 m long.

$2 + 2 + 2 + 2 + 2 = 10$

Check your answer using multiplication.
$2 \times 5 = 10$

12

Solve.

1 Ruby needs 2 m of fabric to make a skirt. How many skirts can she make from 14 m of fabric?

2 m

Ruby can make ☐ skirts.

2 A stack of 10 identical packages is 40 cm tall. What is the height of each package?

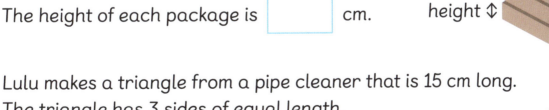

The height of each package is ☐ cm. height ↕

3 Lulu makes a triangle from a pipe cleaner that is 15 cm long. The triangle has 3 sides of equal length. How long is each side?

Each side is ☐ cm.

1 The total mass of a sack of potatoes and a sack of carrots is 18 kg.
The sack of potatoes is 8 kg heavier than the sack of carrots.
What is the mass of the sack of carrots?

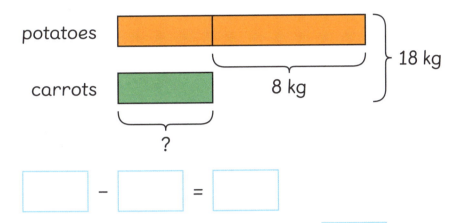

potatoes

carrots   8 kg   18 kg

?

[ ] − [ ] = [ ]

The mass of the sack of carrots is [ ] kg.

2

The skateboard and the scooter have a total mass of 14 kg.
The scooter and the bike have a total mass of 18 kg.
The skateboard weighs 2 kg less than the scooter.
Find the mass of each item.

 [ ] kg    [ ] kg   [ ] kg

Measuring and comparing volume

Sam compares the volume of water in a glass and in a paper cup.

Example

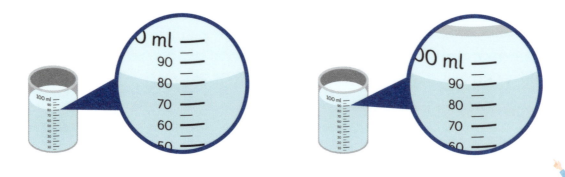

$90 - 80 = 10$

The volume of water in the glass is 80 ml.
The volume of water in the paper cup is 90 ml.

The difference between the volume of water in the glass and the paper cup is 10 ml.

Find the volume of water in each beaker.
Find the difference between the two volumes of water.

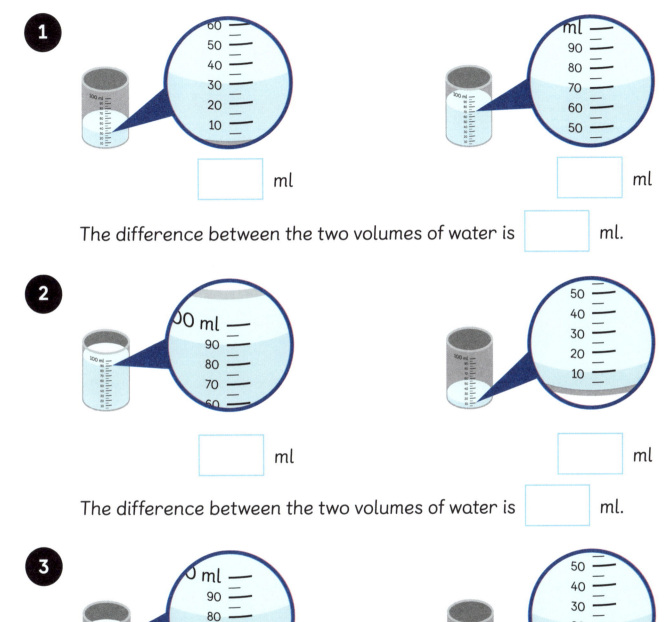

1

60
50
40
30
20
10

[   ] ml

ml
90
80
70
60
50

[   ] ml

The difference between the two volumes of water is [   ] ml.

2

00 ml
90
80
70
60

[   ] ml

50
40
30
20
10

[   ] ml

The difference between the two volumes of water is [   ] ml.

3

0 ml
90
80
70
60
50

[   ] ml

50
40
30
20
10

[   ] ml

The difference between the two volumes of water is [   ] ml.

Answers

Page 5 **1 (a)** 54 **(b)** 34 **2** Answers will vary. **3** 76, 75, 67, 65, 57, 56
4 (a) 54, 59, 63, 72, 77, 85 **(b)** 63 > 59, 77 < 85, 54 < 72, 72 < 77

Page 7 **1 (a)** 37 + 45 = 82. Charles read 82 pages over the two days.

2 56 + 39 = 95. The two classes have 95 books altogether.

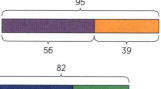

Page 9 **1** 63 – 37 = 26. There are 26 children still in the hall.

2 82 – 48 = 34. 34 children have not yet finished the run.

Page 11 **2** 8 × 10 = 80. The total length of the 10 straws is 80 cm. **2** 5 × 9 = 45. The height of the stack of 9 books is 45 cm. **3** 5 × 7 = 35. The length of the strip of paper was 35 cm to begin with.

Page 13 **1** 14 ÷ 2 = 7. Ruby can make 7 skirts.
2 40 ÷ 10 = 4. The height of each package is 4 cm.

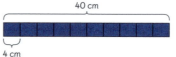

3 15 ÷ 3 = 5. Each side is 5 cm.

Page 15 **1 (a)** Ravi won 12 prizes. **(b)** Ravi won the greatest number of prizes. **(c)** Lulu won the fewest number of prizes. **(d)** The three children won 28 prizes altogether. **2 (a)** The most popular food is lasagne. **(b)** The least popular food is a cheese sandwich. **(c)** 8 more children liked lasagne better than beans on toast. **(d)** 62 children voted altogether.

Page 17 **1 (a)** The restaurant sold 50 tomato salads in one week. **(b)** The restaurant sold 5 fewer cheese salads than chicken salads. **(c)** The restaurant sold 105 salads altogether.
2 (a) Amira has the greatest number of marbles. **(b)** Amira has 10 more marbles than Sam has. **(c)** Holly has 10 fewer marbles than Charles has. **(d)** Charles and Sam have 75 marbles altogether.

Page 19 **1** 40 **2** Year 2 **3** 40 **4** 240

Page 21 **1 (a)** $\frac{1}{3} > \frac{1}{5}$ **(b)** $\frac{1}{5} < \frac{1}{4}$ **(c)** $\frac{3}{4} > \frac{2}{3}$ **(d)** $\frac{2}{3} < \frac{4}{5}$ **2** $\frac{1}{3}, \frac{3}{5}, \frac{2}{3}, \frac{3}{4}$

Page 23 **1**

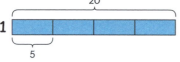

20 ÷ 4 = 5

$\frac{1}{4}$ of 20 is 5

Elliott opens 5 packets of football cards.

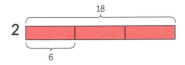

2

$18 \div 3 = 6$

6 children are reading non-fiction books.

3 (a) $24 \div 4 = 6$ $\frac{1}{4}$ of 24 = 6   6 cookies share chocolate chips.

(b) $24 \div 3 = 8$ $\frac{1}{3}$ of 24 = 8   8 cookies have walnuts.

(c) $6 + 8 = 14$ $24 - 14 = 10$ 10 cookies are plain.

Page 25   **1 (a)** $\frac{1}{4}$ of 40 m = 10 m. Ruby puts 10 m of line on her fishing rod.

2 $\frac{1}{3}$ of 15 m = 5 m. Elliott's mum used 5 m of wallpaper.

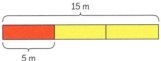

Page 27   **1**

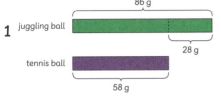

$86 - 28 = 58$

The mass of the tennis ball is 58 g.

2 $6 \div 2 = 3$, $4 - 3 = 1$. The mass of the pineapple is 1 kg.

Page 29   **1 (a)** The  has a mass of 1 kg. **(b)** The has a mass of 4 kg. **(c)** The has a mass of 2 kg. **(d)** The flour is the lightest. **(e)** The rice is the heaviest. **2 (a)** The mass of the coconut is 500 g. **(b)** The mass of the mango is 450 g. **(c)** The mass of the cabbage is 700 g. **(d)** The mango is the lightest. **(e)** The cabbage is the heaviest.

Page 31   **1**

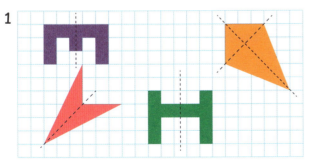

2 Answers will vary.

Page 33   **1** $18 + 15 = 33$. The doll costs £33.

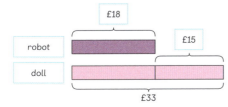

Answers continued

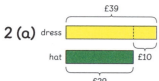

2 (a) 39 − 10 = 29.
The hat costs £29.

(b) 39 + 29 = 68
The dress and the hat cost £68 altogether.

Page 34 **1 (a)** 50p + 25p = 75p. Elliott saves 75p on Monday and Tuesday.

Page 35 **(b)** 75p + 35p = 110p, 110p = £1 and 10p. Elliott saves £1 and 10p over the three days.

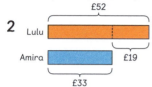

2 52 − 19 = 33

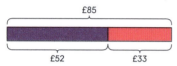

52 + 33 = 85. Lulu and Amira have £85 altogether.

Page 37 **1** 42 + 13 + 22 = 77

100 − 77 = 23
Amira has £23 left.

2

9 + 5 = 14
50 − 14 = 36
The price of the satchel is £36.

Page 39 **1 (a)** (drawing) start time: 5:30, end time: 6:15, duration: 45 min, (swimming) start time: 3:10, end time: 4:00, duration: 50 min **(b)** swimming **(c)** drawing **2 (a)** Lulu started at 4:05. **(b)** Emma started at 4:15. **(c)** Charles spent 55 minutes on his homework.

Page 41 **1** 40 °C, 80 °C, 80 − 40 = 40. The difference between the two temperatures is 40 °C.
2 10 °C, 100 °C, 100 − 10 = 90. The difference between the two temperatures is 90 °C.
3 15 °C, 65 °C, 65 − 15 = 50. The difference between the two temperatures is 50 °C.

Page 43 **1** 18 − 8 = 10. The mass of the sack of carrots is 5 kg.

2
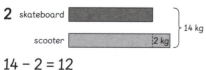
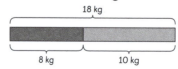

14 − 2 = 12
12 ÷ 2 = 6
skateboard: 6 kg
scooter: 8 kg

18 − 8 = 10
bike: 10 kg

Page 45 **1** 70 − 30 = 40. The difference between the two volumes of water is 40 ml. **2** 90 − 10 = 80. The difference between the two volumes of water is 80 ml. **3** 80 − 20 = 60. The difference between the two volumes of water is 60 ml.